MW01282470

HOW TO
ATTRACT A
GODLY
HUSBAND

Emmanuela Prival Rodenberg

Copyright ©2017 by Emmanuela Prival Rodenberg All rights reserved. No part of this book may be reproduced in any form without the written permission of the author and its publisher.

*I dedicate this book to my parents,
Wilson and Joana Prival.*

*Thank you for all the life lessons about
love and relationships. I am especially
grateful to my dad for teaching me how to
identify, attract, and marry a Godly man.*

ACKNOWLEDGMENTS

This book could not have been possible without the love and support of several people who I love and cherish. First and foremost, I thank God for the gift he placed in me. Thank you, God, for choosing me to be a voice for women—to aid in teaching them how to love you, love themselves, and acquire the relationship of their dreams.

To the love of my life, my husband, Sven Rodenberg. Thank you for your great love and example. Because of you, I can do what I do. You are the man of my dreams. You are the embodiment of God's love for me. Your belief in me inspires me to greatness each day. God knew what I would need in a husband, and he gave me you. I could write pages about you. Thank you for being my greatest inspiration. I want every woman to experience the kind of love you have shown me.

To my pride and joy, my daughters, Hannah and Noelle. I love you more than life itself. It is an honor to be chosen by God to be your mother. Thank you to all my siblings for their love and support—you have taught me so much about unconditional love.

And finally, thank you to my dear friends who believed in me and encouraged me to put my thoughts on paper—you know who you are. Thank you!

CONTENTS

INTRODUCTION

You picked up this book because you're ready to attract a Godly husband, a man who will not only love you but also loves God and desires to please Him in all that He does. I don't know what you've been through—maybe you are just starting to date, and you know from the start you want a Godly man. Perhaps you've been in some relationships that have failed, leaving you confused, hurt and lost. Now, you are ready to learn a new perspective and try a different approach. Whatever position you find yourself in, I hope you will find this book to be an excellent resource. But first, you must have an open mind and an open heart. You must be ready and willing to do some work and apply this new information about how to attract a Godly husband.

My inspiration to write this book came from the unhappy marriages I have witnessed. Growing up, I didn't see many examples of healthy marriages. The marriages I saw didn't inspire me to get married. When you grow up, in an environment one of two things happen: You either end up repeating what you learned from that environment (whether it was good or bad), or you learn from the situation and consciously decide to do something different.

Although my childhood home was not a good example of what marriage was supposed to be, I loved my parents, and I know that they loved my siblings and me. My parents did everything to make sure that we had the opportunity to live the American dream. They provided a home that was happy, healthy, and filled with opportunities for us. Both of my parents worked two jobs to take care of our big family. Their love for us was evident in the support and care they gave us. However, I didn't see evidence of the love my mom and dad had for each other.

I didn't witness a marriage based on love and respect. I grew up telling myself, "If this is what marriage is then I don't ever want to get married." We had fun as a family. My parents did a fine job showing us how to be a solid family unit. To this day, we are close as a family. My parents taught us how to take care of each other and stay connected. We have a strong family bond. It is something I will always be proud of because I know that many families don't experience this.

Though my parents were not a good role model as a married couple, I learned a lot from them. I spent a lot of time with my dad, and though he didn't feel like he had the marriage he wanted, he spent time talking about relationships to my sisters and I. I credit my dad with my interest and knowledge about the dynamics of Godly relationships. He taught me the ways to attract a Godly man. Now, I am going to share with you the core principles on how to attract a Godly man and how I applied them.

CHAPTER 1

START WITH YOU

START WITH YOU

Your Value as a Woman

A man falls in love with a woman's essence, her being, her soul, who she is and who she represents. Let's start by acknowledging how valuable you are as a woman.

> *"A woman who loves and fears God is credited with the highest reward; her noble character directs her heart and actions."*
> *— Proverbs 31:10-31*

> *"To be a God-fearing, gracious, and kind hearted woman is the ultimate victory for a woman in God's kingdom."*
> *— Proverbs 31:29-30*

> *"A wife of noble character is her husband's crown, but a disgraceful wife is like decay in his bones."*
> *— Proverbs 12:4*

> *"A woman who pursues wisdom and Godly character can be the most important influence in a man's life, and an unwise woman can be a man's downfall."*
> *— Emmanuela P. Rodenberg*

Your goal as a woman of God should never be to find a man to marry you. As a daughter of God, you deserve not just to marry any man, but to marry a Godly man—a man who is going to love and cherish you; a man who will put no one above you, other than God.

You deserve a man who shares your values and loves you for those values, a man who truly understands what it means to have virtuous woman by his side. Proverbs 18:22 in the Bible says, "He who finds a wife found a good thing and has obtained favor from God." The man who you choose to marry needs to be a man who knows you are his crown and glory; choose a man who truly knows the value of having the right woman by his side. And remember that important word "choose." Marriage is a choice you make, so it is your responsibility to make an informed one.

Sadly, many women lack the self-confidence to realize how valuable they are. Many women don't realize how much the right man needs them, and that a man is never complete without the right woman by his side. A man doesn't reach his full potential until he is with the right woman. Women are extremely valuable to the right man. Instead of trying to find a man, put your focus on being a Godly woman—be confident in yourself, know your value, and know that you should not accept anything less than what God has created for you. Instead of trying to find who you think is the right man, focus on being the right Godly woman to attract your Godly husband based on God's guidance.

You cannot force a great relationship. We cannot shoulder our way into a man's heart. The bond must be created and ordained by God. The man must come willingly to you. Entering the right relationship is a creative process and shouldn't be rushed.

Allow God to reveal to you—layer by layer and piece by piece—the relationship he has in store for you. Rushing the process will not get you the outcome you desire. There is nothing romantic, fun, or exciting about two people who were never intended to be together getting into a union that God did not create for them. Sadly, most relationships based on this idea ultimately end in divorce.

God does not approve of divorce. He knows the damage it does to people. No matter how it comes about, divorce destroys something in both parties involved. No matter how much we want to ignore it, the divorce rate is high. For every two couples who marry, one will end in divorce. With the divorce rate so high (about 40-50% percent of marriages in the United States end in divorce according to the American Psychological Association), we need to acknowledge that something is happening to cause so many people to change their minds about spending the rest of their lives together.

If you have been through a divorce, God loves you! You are not being punished. He wants you to attract the man you are meant to be with. If you allow Him, He will prepare you for the relationship He has in store for you.

Having a Godly husband starts with the attracting, dating, and selection process. As a society, we are more reactive and not so much proactive. We seek help with our marriages after we have already said "I do," without having a complete understanding of our commitment. As a society, women are enticed to spend money and resources on the wedding day, without investing time and thought in what happens after the ceremony.

So, let's focus on helping you attract and select the right man, how to date, and how to get on track to marrying a Godly man.

The Correct Order of Things

God doesn't give us everything all at once. When God created Adam, He first gave him land, pasture, and animals. He gave Adam resources. Then He said it was not good for man to be alone, and created a mate for him. Take note ladies, Adam had resources before God gave him a woman. A man needs to have resources before you marry him. He needs to have means and a plan on how he is going to take care of you.

God saw the need for Adam to have a mate, not Adam. Adam was content with the Lord's blessings. God needs you to be content with where you are now in your relationship journey. He cannot move you into the next phrase of a relationship until you find joy and contentment where you are right now. The sooner you can find solace and peace in where God has placed you, the sooner he can move you into the next phase. God knows that if you're unfulfilled as a single woman, you will be unfulfilled as a married woman. The secret to contentment is found in God—not in your relationship status.

Adam did not choose Eve. He didn't even realize that he had a need for her. God knew that Adam needed a companion, so He took a piece of Adam to create Eve and brought her to him. God knows what you need, and He will set up and prepare your companion. He will hand-deliver him to you. God's way is the only way for your marriage to be a perfect fit.

So, stop going out on your own and trying to find a man. Wait on God to deliver what he is creating and preparing for you.

God has an order in which He does everything. God must see how we are handling our current blessings before He gives us more. We want a lot of help from God, but God doesn't always give us all the blessings we seek. Often we don't understand that not getting what we want is for our own good. I truly believe when you are a child of God, he doesn't give you anything before you are ready to receive it.

Not everything we have is from God. Sometimes we go out and enter relationships that God didn't intend for us. It was our own doing, and we suffer the consequences of missing or ignoring God's will in our lives.

God must first prepare you before He gives you help, including a Godly husband. You should be prepared emotionally, mentally, spiritually, and physically for a spouse. You don't become prepared when the husband arrives—you must prepare yourself before he arrives. God will make it possible when you trust Him and are obedient to His word.

> *"The highest act of faith is preparation. God can tell what you are expecting by what you are doing."*
> *—Emmanuela P. Rodenberg*

How are you preparing yourself for the blessings you are asking God for? It could be letting go of a relationship that is not right for you, or letting go of the need for a physical relationship outside of marriage. It could be surrounding yourself with friends who support a healthy lifestyle instead of going out to bars every night. What can you be doing now? Start honoring your body and save it for marriage. Next, think about other tasks you can accomplish to get yourself ready for your husband.

*"For my thoughts are not your thoughts, neither
are your ways my ways, declares the Lord."*
— *Isaiah 55:8*

Our way is not God's way. God knows what He is doing. He doesn't need our help. Stop telling God how to do His job. He has got this! Trust and know that He's got your back. You have to move out of the way and allow Him to be the God of your life. He doesn't always do things how we think they should be done or when we think they should be done. As women, we grow up having an idea of how and when events are supposed to happen for us romantically. We've envisioned how we are going to meet our Prince Charming; how he'll sweep us off our feet, and we'll ride off into the sunset together, living happily ever after. But God has his vision and plan for us, which often is different than how we planned.

*"We can make our plans, but the
Lord determines our steps."*
— *Proverbs 16:9*

I always had a dream of traveling and experiencing life in different cities, states, and countries. After graduating college and working for a few years, I decided to start my adventure. I moved to a different state and started exploring. I moved to three different states in five years. I was living my dream. Little did I know at the time that God was ordering my steps.

*"The Lord makes firm the steps of the
one who delights in Him."*
—*Psalm 37:23*

God was ordering my steps even when I didn't know where I was going. I didn't know where the right place was. I didn't live a perfect life, but God was my guide. God already knew where I was going before I set out on my adventure.

> *"From one man God made every nation of men,*
> *that they should inhabit the whole earth; and*
> *He determined the times set for them and the*
> *exact places where they should live."*
> *—Acts 17:26*

God is in control of all things. He already knows what we are going to do before we do it. Before I left home, God already knew where I would live, the people I would meet, and the experiences I would have.

Growing up, I had a vision of my husband in my head. I imagined my fairy tale wedding and the happy ending I would have. I imagined dancing every night with my husband. I thought he would be from the Caribbean because I love zouk music. I would never have believed that a girl from Haiti would meet a German man in Birmingham, Alabama. What are the odds? But that's exactly what happened.

> *"Eye has not seen, nor ear heard, nor have*
> *entered into the heart of man the things which*
> *God has prepared for those who love Him."*
> *—1 Corinthians 2:9*

God has bigger and better dreams for us than we can ever dream for ourselves. That's what He did when He joined my husband and me. God knew I wanted to see the world, so He gave me an international man who loves to travel. He has taken me on adventures around the world. God sure knows how to spoil a girl!

CHAPTER 2

THE ULTIMATE
TRUST FACTOR

THE ULTIMATE
TRUST FACTOR

"Trust in the Lord with all your heart,
and do not lean on your own understanding,
in all your ways acknowledge Him and
He will make your path straight."
—Proverbs 3:5

Who do you trust? Yourself or God? You must be clear on that from the beginning. If you place all trust in yourself, then the process outlined in this book is not for you. If you trust in God, then you must trust that He will withhold no good thing from you. He longs to give you the desires of your heart if you trust and have unwavering faith. Trust and faith go hand in hand. You can't have one without the other.

"Now, faith is the substance of things
hoped for, the evidence of things not seen."
—Hebrews 11:1

Think back over your life and remember times when God has come through for you in your career, health, networking, finances, safety, family, and friendships. These assets are His divine, unmerited favor.

Think of all you have now. Who gave them to you? If you know God has done all this for you, then you are in the right place. If God has been with you all your life, ordering your steps, blessing you, protecting you, and keeping you, why wouldn't you trust Him with one of the most important decisions your life? This union is your destiny, your family line. After the decision to make Jesus the Lord of your life, deciding on the man you marry is the second most important decision you will ever make.

You didn't pick up this book accidentally. It is the next step for you. You are getting ready to attract the right man into your life. A true man of God. No imitations. I know there are no guarantees, that's just a fact of life. But when God is in control, and you truly seek and wait on Him, He is going to do the choosing. He knows what you need. He won't fail you. Not to say that you won't have any tough times because you will. That's normal. But God is with you, and that's the best guarantee.

Your First Love

Everyone remembers their first love. There is something magical about falling in love for the first time. It's intense: it's exciting. You can't wait to be with that person. Just the thought of them puts a smile on your face and butterflies in your stomach. You want to spend every waking moment with them. You are joyful, full of hope for the future. There's nothing you won't do for that person. There is something special about that first love which leaves a lasting impression on us.

There is another first love that I want to introduce you to if you don't already know about Him. It's Jesus Christ; he is the creator of first loves and love itself. In fact, He is love. So, before we can even get to talking about how to attract a Godly husband, we must get to know God and fall in love with God, the creator of love. You cannot skip this step. People think they can skip over this part and have a positive outcome. But in my opinion, it's too much of a gamble. Why would you leave out the person who created what you are trying to attain? Why not go to the person who invented love to get all your questions answered? God longs to give you the desires of your heart, but first He must have your heart. He created love; therefore, He knows all about it. In fact, He gives us a great definition of what love is and what it's not in the book of Corinthians:

> *"Love is patient, love is kind. It does not envy, it does not boast, it is not proud. It does not dishonor others, it is not self-seeking, it is not easily angered, it keeps no record of wrongs. Love does not delight in evil but rejoices with the truth. It always protects, always trusts, always hopes, always perseveres. Love never fails."*
> — *Corinthians 13:4-8*

What is Your Definition of Love?

Love can show up uniquely for many people. Whatever you might be looking for when it comes to love, you cannot redefine the foundation for a Godly love. We should trust that God had reasons for His definition of love. We must trust that He knows these are the elements we will need for us to have authentic intimacy, passion, and longevity in our relationships.

The definition of love cannot be modified to fit your situation—it is love, or it's not. God is not going to change his definition of love to fit your circumstance. You must change your situation to align with what God says love is.

Don't change your definition of love just because you want to be in a relationship that you know deep down is clearly not love. Is what you're calling love, actually love? Be honest with yourself. If you're in a relationship that is not love, at what point did you decide this is the best God can do. Why are you limiting God? Why are you settling for less than you know you deserve, for something that is not love? Why are you afraid to hold out for real, Godly love? Do you believe in love? Do you know what love is supposed to look and feel like? How will you know when it shows up? Having a deeply intimate relationship with your Creator will ensure that you attract a Godly man. When you are about God's business, He takes care of you and orders your steps. God knows all about you; He created you. He knows things about you that you haven't yet discovered.

> *"Before I formed you in the womb I knew you,*
> *before you were born I set you apart; I appointed*
> *you as a prophet to the nations."*
> *— Jeremiah 1:5*

God knows you intimately. Every inch of you He knitted together in your mother's womb. No one else knows you more intimately than God because He made you. You need to get to know Him so He can reveal intimate information about you to yourself. My prayer for every woman reading this book is that they will take the time to get to know Christ and trust He will give you a man after His own heart.

> *"I pray that out of His glorious riches He may*
> *strengthen you with power through his Spirit in your*
> *inner being, so that Christ may dwell in your hearts*
> *through faith. And I pray that you, being rooted and*
> *established in love, may have power, together with all*
> *the Lord's holy people, to grasp how wide and long and*
> *high and deep is the love of Christ, and to know this*
> *love that surpasses knowledge—that you may be filled to*
> *the measure of all the fullness of God."*
> *—Ephesians 3:16-19*

CHAPTER 3

GOD KNOWS YOU

GOD KNOWS YOU

What Does God Know About You?

God knows your inner being. He knows what you need because He made you to desire certain things. God knows what you will need in a spouse to have a great, loving, and lasting marriage. He knows your insecurities, your flaws, your weaknesses; He knows all the challenges coming your way. The Bible promises us that we will have tribulations. So, when God creates a spouse for you, He has all those objectives in mind. You will lack nothing you need.

As I look back over the years with my husband, I'm glad God had His hand in my choosing. We have a great marriage by the grace of God, but we are not free from troubles. We have two beautiful daughters after losing many other angels. But I can honestly say that God handpicked my husband knowing what the future would have in store for us. We've faced many challenges together, and with each challenge, we have grown closer. There was no way I could have known what challenges we would face, but God did, and He made provision beforehand.

Many couples grow apart with challenges, but God has allowed tough times to bring us closer to Him and each other. The real test of love is not when everything is going right but when challenges arise. How you handle them together as a couple will determine the future of your union.

I didn't fully understand why God gave me this man as my husband until I was in the hospital losing our first son, Christof. It was one of the scariest times in my life. I was lying in a hospital bed losing our baby and feeling like my world was coming to an end. My husband never left my side; he gave me sponge baths and massaged my back. He was strong when I couldn't be. There was no doubt that this man loved me from the bottom of his heart. I had no doubt that he was from God. We have faced many other challenges, and he has been by my side every step of the way. Through miscarriages, five months of bed rest, and losing both of our mothers. People can't believe how incredible my husband is, and most times, I can't believe how incredibly blessed I am that God chose such an awesome man for me.

The key here is choice: when we make a choice, and don't wait on God, we are making decisions based on limited information. This is why I believe so many marriages are failing; people are impatient. They are going out and "choosing" their mates. It baffles me how lightly some women take such a huge decision, a decision that can alter the course of their lives and generations to come.

Attracting and choosing a Godly man is one of the most important decisions you will ever make. It should be done with lots of prayer and careful considerations from trusted love ones. It is not a decision you want to make on an impulse or lack of patience. As the saying goes, it's better to be single and wishing you were married than to be married and wishing you were single.

CHAPTER 4

LOVE YOURSELF

CHAPTER 4

LOVE YOURSELF

"Love starts with you loving yourself."
—Emmanuela P. Rodenberg

No one will love you more than you love yourself, unless they are your parents. I know this first hand. I had a difficult time loving myself growing up. It started from childhood, which is typically where women learn what love is and how love is experienced. At a very young age, I never felt pretty enough. I had a lot of insecurities. I was teased because I didn't fit the definition of beauty. It wasn't until I began to love the person I was that my self-confidence increased, and others started to notice. I learned an important lesson early on— directly or indirectly; we tell people how to treat us and how valuable we are based on how we treat ourselves and the value we place on ourselves. We are our first love; we must learn to see our beauty before expecting others to see it. And when we meet a man, we tell him how we expect to be treated and how valuable we are by how we value and treat ourselves.

Who Are You?

A crucial part in attracting a Godly husband is you knowing who you are. The way to know who you are is by getting to know the person who created you. I can't tell you how many times I've tried to get around this step. I started comparing it to having a new phone or a new car. We want the latest and fanciest gadgets. We walk around with them unaware of their full potential. Unless you take the time to read the manuals, watch a video, or ask the professionals, you will never reap all the advantages of having the most technologically advanced phone or car.

So, unless you spend time with your Maker, getting to know how you were created and what you were created to do, you will never know your full potential. If you don't know your full potential, you are selling yourself short in your relationships. Don't you think you have more potential than a new phone or car? So, take some time. Read your manual, read the Bible, get to know God. Understand why He made you and discover the amazing things you can do.

The best time to get to know yourself and discover your full potential is when you are single. Relationships are great, but they can cloud our judgment and distract us from our core purpose. We can use a relationship to hide from reality and avoid discovering who we truly are. When that happens, we look to our partner for validation; asking, "Do you think I'm pretty? Do you think I'm talented? What do you think my gifts and talents are? Do you believe in me? Do you think I'm valuable?" We find ourselves desperately looking for answers from someone else when we should find those answers within ourselves.

When you don't know who you are in a relationship, you become an accessory to your partner's dreams and visions. You become a part of their journey, whether you want to or not. You become a tag-along, an extra, a bonus—but you are an asset on your own! You have dreams and aspirations. You are worth more than just following someone else's dreams. You should take the time to dream your dreams and discover what God has in store for you. God has a divine purpose for you. You want to be a whole person and bring value to any relationship you are in because you know who you are, have a life vision, and understand God's purpose for your life.
So, before we go any further, take a few minutes to answer the questions below truthfully. Use more than "yes" or "no" answers. Give an honest statement for each question you are asking yourself. It is your self-assessment.

Get a pencil or a pen, and write your answers here, on these pages. This is more than a book; it is your journal.

Discovering Your Inner Truth

- How have I taken the time to understand my real essence as a woman?

- What are my strengths and weaknesses?

- What is my value in a relationship?

- How do I take responsibility for the relationships I have had?

• How do I show I am worthy of love and total acceptance?

- How do I show that respect starts with me?

- Give an example of how your wants and needs differ in your life.

- What is the clear vision for my life and relationships?

- How do I showcase I am a woman of excellence?

- What am I happy for in my life right now?

- How can I become more comfortable being alone with myself?

- How do I know I am ready to commit emotionally?

- What do I want in a partner?

- What do I need in a partner?

- What are my core values?

- What are my non-negotiables for a healthy relationship?

• How do I spend time daily with God?

- How do I continuously strive to become my best self?

If it was difficult for you to answer any of the previous questions, then take time to pause and think. Take your time and answer them. Don't rush. Consider each question and be clear about your answers. They will be your guide. Writing out your answers to the questions in the book makes your commitment to this process more real. So, if you need to take a break, do that. For an hour, a day, or however long you need to truthfully and fully respond. Remember, you are worth taking the time to know yourself more, to know what you want and need. And until you do, you can't take the next steps with pure intention.

> *"A woman cannot successfully pick the right husband*
> *for herself without first knowing who she is."*
> —*Emmanuela P. Rodenberg*

Let's continue, and take the questions a step further:

• What makes you stand out?

- What makes you irresistible?

- What is your sexy factor?

- What makes you an asset to the man you are desiring?

- What do you have to offer that no other woman can?

You must be able to answer these questions and be confident in your responses. You must know yourself before you can identify the right man for you. You have to know your shoe size before you buy shoes, or your feet will hurt because you chose the wrong size! You can save a lot of time, stress, and disappointment if you take the time to measure yourself properly. In this case, doing the work on yourself and getting to know yourself is key to understanding what you need and want in a mate.

Take Care of Yourself

Once you know who you are, take care of yourself. How are you handling the first person God entrusted you with? How are you nurturing yourself? How are you taking care of you?

Every woman needs a self-care program. How are you replenishing yourself? How are you staying connected to God and allowing Him to be the center of your life? How are you staying sane in such a busy world? How are you staying vibrant, beautiful, and rejuvenated? Part of loving yourself is taking care of yourself! What is your daily regimen? What makes you feel good about yourself?

The answers are different for every woman, but there are some common things we all should be doing for self-care:

- Get restful sleep—Have a designated bedtime to make sure you are getting enough rest for your mind and body.

- Devote daily time with God—I recommend doing this in the morning before you jump into your day. Get up an hour earlier than normal and have a quiet time with God.

- Pray and read your Bible. Write all your prayers, concerns, desires, and anything that is weighing on your mind in a journal.

- Exercise daily—This could be as easy as taking the stairs at work or going for a walk to clear your mind.

- Eat nutritious meals.

- Connect with loved ones.

- Have fun—Take 15-30 minutes a day and do something just for pure enjoyment. Sing, dance, nap, meditate, take a bath, watch your favorite show, listen to music, or whatever makes you smile.

If you are currently doing all or some of these tasks, great! If you are not currently doing any of these things, start small by picking one or two things to start. Take notice of how you feel actively practicing these activities. Slowly incorporate more self-care into your daily regimen until you feel you are taking great care of yourself. Starting today, find something you can do to nourish yourself. Remember, you won't be able to successfully nurture another person if you are not actively nurturing yourself.

CHAPTER 5

WANTS VS. NEEDS– IT'S ALL IN THE DETAILS

WANTS VS. NEEDS–
IT'S ALL IN THE
DETAILS

Now that you have taken the time to discover who you are and nurture yourself, it's time to become clear about what you want, what you don't want, and most importantly, what you need in a husband. Let's break them down into four categories:

1. Your must-haves
2. Your nice-to-haves
3. Your not-so-importants
4. Your don't-needs and don't-wants

These needs are based on knowing your core values. Where are you unwilling to compromise? What means more to you than being in a relationship? What gives your life meaning? Define what you can't live without. You should consider all these things when making your list of must haves.

1. My Top 5 Must-Haves

For me, it was essential that the man I married loved and feared God. I wanted the man I would marry to have a solid relationship with God. I wanted him to know that he was accountable to God first, not just to me. I know that I'm not a perfect person and neither is he. I would upset him at some point, and he would not always be happy with me. In those times, I needed him to remember his commitment to God. He should do the right thing primarily because of his love for God, and then because of his love for me.

It was essential that we love each other's family. I have a close relationship with my family. We spend a lot of time together, and I wanted my spouse to be a part of that. I wanted him to love and fit into my family. I also wanted to love and fit into his family. I was tired of hearing people complain about their in-laws and how dreadful it was for them every time they had to spend time together. I didn't want that. I prayed that I would love my in-laws even before I was married. I love my in-laws, and my husband loves my family. We are a large Haitian family. We can be a bit overwhelming for him at times, but ultimately, he truly loves them.

Another must-have was for my husband to be a man of integrity and trustworthiness. A healthy relationship cannot exist without trust. It was non-negotiable. I needed to be able to trust my man and know that his "yes" meant "yes" and his "no" meant "no." I couldn't be with a man that might lie, cover up the truth, leave things out, or deceive me in any way.

Look back at your previous answers and take some more time to identify your must-haves and your reasons why. Your why's should be so strong that you are not willing to compromise them for anyone.

Write a list of 5 of your must-haves here:

1. ....

2. ....

3. ....

4. ....

5. ....

2. My Nice-to-Haves

These are the attributes you don't need to have but would be nice to have. They are not deal-breakers; rather, they are things you want, or wouldn't mind having, but don't necessarily need. Seeking a man in a certain income bracket—while some women might say it's a must, having a man who makes a lot of money doesn't guarantee you a fulfilling marriage. I remember my dad always telling me, "Don't be impressed with what a man has before you, find out how he attained it." It's better to work and build a life with someone rather than marrying into his riches. It creates a better partnership. Wealth in love is much more important to a healthy marriage than money in a bank account.

Write a list of 5 of your nice-to-haves here:

1. _____

2. _____

3. _____

4. _____

5. _____

3. Things That Are Just Not That Important

And if they are not that important, why are we even talking about them? Because some women make life decisions on these not-so-importants. A not-so-important thing might be wanting a man with six-pack abs, a man who dresses a particular way, or a man of a certain race. We all have our certain preferences, which is fine. But I think what's most important is asking yourself, "Are these requirements going to increase my chances of having a strong, loving, and successful marriage?"

When you are choosing a forever life partner, you should base it on qualities that are more permanent, such as character, values, and integrity instead of things that can easily be altered like appearance and style. These are not key ingredients for a successful marriage.

Write a list of 5 not-so-important things here:

1. ....
2. ....
3. ....
4. ....
5. ....

4. Things I Do Not Need And Do Not Want

Lastly, what are some things that you do not want in a spouse, things you are not willing to compromise on. It could be that you don't want someone who smokes. Remember, these are things that you do not want and do not need.

My top 5 don't-need and don't-wants:

1. ....
2. ....
3. ....
4. ....
5. ....

Now, look back at your answers for this 4-step exercise. These lists will help you recognize the right guy for you when he comes along.

How to Identify What You Need

"But the Lord said to Samuel, 'Do not consider his appearance or his height, for I have rejected him. The Lord does not look at the things people look at. People look at the outward appearance, but the Lord looks at the heart.'"

—1 Samuel 16:7

Most people look at outside appearance. God looks at the heart. What are you looking at? Muscles, fashion style, and good looks are all external attributes. Not to say that these things don't matter—they do to an extent, but they are not the main things you should look at when you want a husband for life. Take your eyes off the external and fix your eyes on the internal. What is on the inside? What are his core values? What are his goals and aspirations? What is dear to his heart? What is his true character?

"The true test of a man's character is what he does when no one is watching."
—John Wooden

John Wooden was an American basketball player who won 10 NCAA national championships in a 12-year period as head coach at UCLA, known for his "Seven Point Creed." He encourages us to be more concerned with a person's character than their reputation because a person's character is who they are, while their reputation is merely what others think of them.

Attributes You Should Be Looking At

- What are the man's top 3 character traits?

_____

....

_____

- What are the man's self-care regimens?

....

_____

....

- What are the man's non-negotiables?

....

_____

....

- What is the man's passion?

....

....

_____

- What are the man's values?

_____

....

_____

- What does the man treasure?

- Who does the man surround himself with?

- Who are the man's trusted advisors?

These are some of the important qualities you should be focused on when choosing a husband. These qualities are what attracted me to my husband. The man to be my husband wasn't my type. We all have a certain type in mind, right? It wasn't until after I spent time with him in a group that I noticed his character, and it was at that moment he got my attention. A group of us were hanging out, having light conversation about life and relationships when someone in the group asked my future husband a question about his ex-girlfriend. The way he answered the question with kindness and respect showed me that he was a man of good character, that he respected women, and that I could trust he would respect me. Of course, I didn't make my decision solely on that, but it certainly was a starting point for me.

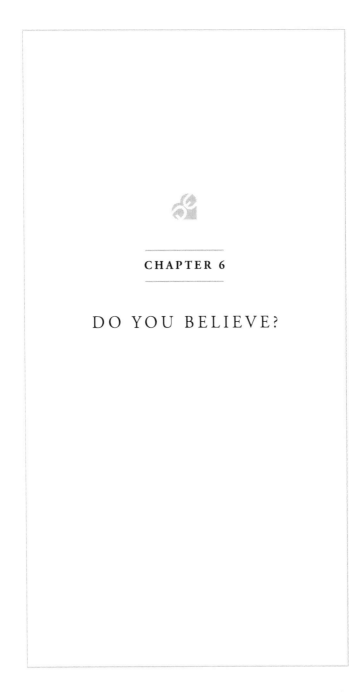

CHAPTER 6

DO YOU BELIEVE?

DO YOU BELIEVE?

We don't get what we want, we get what we believe we deserve. It's not enough to just want a Godly husband. You should believe that God is going to send you one. Your belief system plays a big part in the man who you attract and choose. You must believe without a doubt. Hold out and trust that God will come through.

> *"For truly I tell you, if you have faith the size of a mustard seed, you will say to this mountain, 'Move from here to there,' and it will move; and nothing will be impossible for you."*
> *—Matthew 17:20-21*

> *"Delight yourself in the Lord and he will give you the desires of your heart."*
> *—Psalm 37:4*

A few pages ago, you made some lists. Now, make a list of everything you're looking for in a spouse. You don't need to fill out the list completely. We will get to that next...

A Summary of What I am Looking For In a Spouse

1. ....
2. ....
3. ....
4. ....
5. ....
6. ....
7. ....
8. ....
9. ....
10. ....

Additional Attributes

....

....

....

....

....

....

....

....

"When I was a child, I talked like a child, I thought like a child, I reasoned like a child. When I became a man (woman), I put the ways of childhood behind me."
— *Corinthians 13:11*

Let's go back and add some things to your list. You are a mature woman. You are ready to attract the right man into your life. Let's talk about a few things you might want to add to your list if they are not already there: God-fearing, integrity, honesty, trustworthy, compassionate, kind, respectful, well-mannered, generous, and responsible.

The dreams we had as little girls of our Prince Charming and our wedding dress are lovely dreams. These dreams are important because that is where it all starts. As we mature and view life from a new perspective, we must have a clear visual of what we want in a spouse, and more importantly, what we want life to look like in this relationship. Here is where most women struggle—they are stuck in the Hollywood movie fantasy. They don't think beyond the handsome guy and the wedding day.

To help you get clear about the future spouse you are envisioning, we are going to do another exercise, but this time you do not need a pen or pencil.

An Exercise in Envisioning

I want you to find a quiet place where you feel relaxed. Go to another room in your house, or maybe outside in your yard, or any special place that's just yours. Somewhere that's your sanctuary; a place where you feel safe and secure. Go to your happy place! Once you find that place, find a spot, have a seat and get comfortable. We are going to clear your mind of all the busyness of life so that you can come to place where you are focused on joy and peace.

Now, close your eyes, take a deep breath, and hold it for eight seconds, exhale slowly, releasing every stressed, toxic thought out of your mind. Do these three more times.

Once you are totally relaxed, let's start envisioning the life that you want for yourself. This exercise might be hard for some. Not everyone can allow themselves to completely relax and visualize. Some of you might not even know what you want to create. Close your eyes anyway. Give it your best effort.

Now, I want you to imagine your life 10 years from now. You are living your dream life; there are no limitations and no restrictions. Your world is perfect in your mind. Envision your ideal life. Who is with you? What are you doing? What kind of impact are you having on the world? What has you smiling? What is causing the sparkle in your eyes?

Imagine you are married to your dream spouse. Think about him, describe him in your mind. I'm there with you, a friend who you are casually sharing your thoughts with. What is his name? How tall is he? What color are his eyes? What color is his hair? Describe the look in his eyes when he looks at you. Describe his smile. Tell me about his personality. Is he funny? Serious? What attracted you to him? What made him stand out to you? Describe his character. Is he trustworthy? Reliable? Do you feel safe and protected with him? Are you your best self with him? How do you feel when you are with him? Does he inspire you? Do you feel supported by him? Are you at ease when he's around? What is your favorite thing about him? Why is he the one?

Tell me about your life together. What do you like to do together? What are your favorite things to do for fun? What do you have in common? Do you feel cherished by him? What does he love about you? Who are you when you're with him? Are you comfortable being the real you with him?

If this is too much to do right now, don't worry. Don't rush the process. Maybe take a break, take a walk, then come back and allow yourself to get back into living in that moment. Feel it, embrace it, own it. Allow yourself to enjoy the experience of living your ideal life with the man of your dreams.

When you're ready, allows yourself to come out of your dream state. I want you to remember the experience you just had. The excitement, the joy, and the happiness you experienced—keep these emotions in the forefront of your mind. Believe it is possible to attract that kind of love into your life. Believe that it is going to happen.

Now that you have experienced what life can be like with the man of your dreams, let's talk about how to attract the Godly husband into your life.

LET GOD BE YOUR GUIDE

CHAPTER 7

LET GOD BE YOUR GUIDE

Attracting a Godly man into your life requires patience and discernment. Both attributes come from God. It is impossible to have a Godly relationship with a man outside of your relationship with God. Discernment is important; otherwise, how will you know if he is truly a man of God? We all know people who thought they were marrying a Godly man, but it turned out that person was an impostor. How can anyone know for sure?

> *"Who, then, is the man that fears the Lord? He will instruct him in the way chosen for him. He will spend his days in prosperity, and his descendants will inherit the land. The Lord confides in those who fear him; he makes his covenant known to them. My eyes are ever on the Lord, for only he will release my feet from the snare."*
> *—Psalms 25:12-15*

I love this scripture! God wants us to have reverence for Him and fear Him. And by fear, God does not mean for us to be afraid. It's more like respecting Him and honoring His guidance. He is ready to instruct you and lead you to what He has in store for you. So, you don't have to worry about being deceived if you truly surrender to His guidance with a pure and trusting heart. God will instruct you, confide in you and order your steps.

Is God Listening?

Have you ever asked yourself, "Does God listen to me or hear me? Why do all my friends have husbands and love except me? Why do I keep getting my heart broken? Why am I still alone?"

"Surely the arm of the Lord is not too short to save, nor his ear too dull to hear. But your iniquities have separated you from your God; your sins have hidden his face from you, so that he will not hear."
—Isaiah 59:1

"He who cannot be advised can also not be helped."
—Italian proverb

If you are a single woman who desires to be married, or if you're divorced and have been single for a while, you might wonder if God hears your prayers for the right husband. It can be hard to sit and wait, especially if your friends and other singles around you are getting married. It can be a letdown, and you might find yourself feeling depressed and saddened. You might start to let your mind wonder, "What's wrong with me? Why can everyone seem to find love except me?"

I encourage you to take heart because God has not forgotten about you. He is concerned about you, and He cares deeply for you. But God is also a jealous God. He doesn't want you putting anything or anyone before Him. So, no matter how badly you want to be in a relationship, God has to know that you value your relationship with Him first, above any other relationship. You must get to a place where your relationship with God is enough for you.

It's hard, I know, but you must first surrender to God's will. You must get to a place where you can accept whatever He chooses for you. As hard as that might be, you have to surrender and trust that God knows what's best for you even if that means being single for much longer than you want to be.

I want to teach you how to attract a Godly man and also share my relationship with God. I want you to know how He has worked in my life. There is great peace in surrendering! It's the most freeing thing you can do. It takes the pressure off you and puts it in God's hands, right where it belongs. Try to totally surrender this matter to God and see what happens next. My greatest blessings have come after I've surrendered.

CHAPTER 8

PREPARING BY GETTING YOUR LIFE IN ORDER

PREPARING BY GETTING YOUR LIFE IN ORDER

God is your rescue, not a man! Stop waiting for a man to save you. First, rescue yourself. You should have your life under control before a man comes along. I know too many women who are waiting for the right guy to come along to rescue them from their lives—to save them from sadness, loneliness, or boredom. A man should know you want him because you love him, not because you need him to rescue you from your mess. You must be willing to face your chaos, fears, and insecurities and not simply want a man to come to your rescue. You should be a whole woman on your own. You cannot be desperately seeking love. You should be ok with being alone. You might find a man who you think will rescue you, but sooner or later he is going to realize he can't rescue you from yourself. You then become a burden he must carry, and this leads to an unhealthy, unbalanced relationship that will crumble.

I know a lot of women who feel broken and insecure because of things that happened in their childhood or past relationships. Instead of working on themselves and analyzing their brokenness, they go from relationship to relationship trying to mend themselves only to discover they come out of every relationship more broken and insecure than before.

As women, we must understand that we are responsible for our happiness. A man can add to your joy—he cannot be the only source of happiness. I said it before, and I will say it again, God should be the source of your joy and happiness.

I encourage you to get yourself in order before entering a serious relationship. You should be okay with the person you are now and the person you are becoming. We all have flaws. We all have elements of ourselves we are always trying to improve upon. Constant learning is part of being alive and evolving into more mature and wise women of the world.

The issues I'm talking about here are the problems you think will just go away if you had the right man. Think about it.

If you've been running away from your past, you should stop and face whatever it is that you are running away from. You must know that as long as you are running, it will always chase you. You know the saying: "Wherever you go, there you are." The moment you stop and truly face it, deal with it, and make peace with it, the problem no longer has power over you. Until you do that, you are just carrying baggage from one relationship to the next and wondering why you keep getting the same outcome. It's because you take yourself with you in every relationship that you enter.

So, if you want to see something different, you must be different. It always goes back to you. You determine the quality of the relationships in your life with the quality time you spend working on yourself. You must be whole and confident. Don't see yourself as a victim but as someone who is stable, content, and at peace with yourself. There's no shortcut. You should be willing to put in the work. You will need some help so don't hesitate to reach out and find a qualified person to help you. Whether it's me, a close girlfriend, a church counselor, or a medical therapist, reach out if you need to. It's ok. In fact, it's more than ok. It shows you're ready to take care of yourself so you can attract a Godly husband!

Be Busy Living Your Life—Don't Wait

I met my husband while I was living my life. I wasn't waiting around and looking for a boyfriend. Your husband will find you while you are busy living the life God called you to live. Your life shouldn't be put on hold until a husband comes along. Live your life now! While you are busy enjoying life, a wonderful man will come along. I know it's a cliché, but it's true. It will happen when you're not looking. I was following my dreams, traveling and experiencing the world. This approach is critical. A woman must be fully satisfied with being single before getting married. Now is the time for you to do what you desire. Go on adventures to discover what you like. Travel with your girlfriends. Join an organization that supports a cause you care about. Play a sport. Learn a foreign language, learn a craft, get a hobby, do volunteer work, attend social events, get involved in your community, make new friends. It can be scary to jump in, but there is so much to do. Do some or do it all, just do something. Don't sit around waiting. Go out and live your life!

Many women believe being married is going to complete them and fill all the empty space in their lives. Let me tell you; it will not! You should already feel good about who you are, know your value, be joyful, be fun, and all the things you think the relationship will provide. If you don't bring these qualities with you into the relationship, you won't be building on a solid foundation. Enjoy the stage you are at. Learn and prepare yourself for what's to come. Get busy living the life you envisioned for yourself. Then, you'll be standing on a solid foundation when your Godly husband comes along, and you won't have any doubts or insecurities. You will be a whole person. You will be ready.

The Big Secret

So, what are the secrets to attracting a Godly husband? You already know: Seek God, know yourself, love yourself, be content with your single-hood, work on yourself, be confident, know your value, live life, be joyful, and be happy.

The main ingredient is being the type of person you are seeking. Godly men are attracted to Godly women who are confident, respectful and value themselves. Women who are caring, kind, compassionate, friendly, and fun attract these same men! Remember the lists you made about what you're looking for in a husband? Well, that's what a Godly man is looking for in a wife, too!

CHAPTER 9

CHOOSE WISELY!
BE SELECTIVE

CHOOSE WISELY!
BE SELECTIVE

"Choose your life's mate carefully. From this one decision will come 90 percent of all your happiness or misery."

—H. Jackson Brown, Jr., the American author best known for Life's Little Instruction Book

"Marriage was designed to be a one-time event with no do-overs."
—Emmanuela P. Rodenberg

How would you choose a spouse if you truly believe in the sanctity of marriage? This man is the person you must spend the rest of your life with, in sickness and in health, for richer or poorer, for better or worse till death do you part. If divorce and separation were not an option and happiness was mandatory, how much thought would you put into choosing your life partner?

A lot of people choose their life partners with the back door exit in mind. If things don't work out, they can always leave. You are setting yourself up for failure before the marriage begins. There is no back door; there's not even a window. We can do a better job in choosing the right spouse for ourselves, and I think we would if we didn't leave the back door open. Sometimes divorce is necessary. I do not advise women to stay in a marriage where they don't feel safe or are being abused.

People close to me have gotten married, believing the man was the right man. Sadly, some of those marriages didn't last. One person may have betrayed the other. Or one may have changed their character so much that the relationship became toxic and irredeemable. That's ok, that's part of life. You're not a bad person. If you're reading this book, you want to change. You want to understand. You want to learn. The work should be done before the marriage, not after you say, "I do." If you've been married before, you can start over. If you're married now and are unsure of your marriage's stability, you can try to rebuild with the principles outlined here. If you've never been married, start with the process in this book, and your foundation will be substantial.

Marriage requires work just like anything else we expect to be great. My husband and I are not always laughing and hugging. Marriage is about conversation and compromise; it is hard sometimes. There are disagreements. There are days you just want to pull your hair out. But that's true for everything worth attaining, whether it's a skill like playing the piano or learning a new software program for your job. It takes work. No one becomes great at something without working hard at it. Marriage is no different—it's two people coming together and becoming one. There should be sacrifices made by both parties for the union to work, for both people to feel loved, valued, and respected. But all the work in the world won't help if you don't choose the right person from the start. It is possible to help a man change his ways, but that rarely happens. It's so much easier if you just choose the right person from the beginning.

Inviting God into your life from the start is essential, but you also should be active with the wisdom God gives you. Choosing the right man is not solely a heart decision—it's a head decision, too. When choosing a life partner, you should rely more on your head than your heart. The head should be leading the heart. You can't simply rely on the heart. The heart can get confused. The heart makes decisions based on emotions which change regularly. So use both. Pay close attention to what your head is telling you, follow your gut and your intuition.

A man may not always tell you who he is, but he will always show you. Listen to his words carefully and watch his actions. Do they match up? Does he do what he says he will do? Or does he "talk the big talk" and never follow through? Look into your head, your heart, and your spirit. Are you at peace? Are you anxious? Are you doubtful? Are you willing to bet your life on this person? That's what you are doing. You are going to be putting your life in this person's hands. You should be sure, and you will need some help to determine that he is the one.

As women, we can over-complicate things. We were born with a great intuition. If you listen to your intuition, it will keep you out of getting involved in the wrong relationships. We have an inner guide that God is always using to speak to us, but, we are not always listening and paying attention. As women, we should learn how to ask the right questions and pay attention to the answers we receive. Allow people who love you to help you assess. Often, others can see things that you cannot.

You Can't Turn the Wrong Guy into the Right Guy

Sometimes we can be fooled by a guy who pretends to be someone he isn't. He may be charming and handsome. He might compliment you all the time and make all kinds of promises. That's why we must always be alert. No one is perfect. Sometimes even the smartest women can be fooled by a liar. Early in the relationship, men typically show signs of how it will be in the future. When a man does things early in the relationship, there is a strong possibility he will do it again later. When you're dating, that is the best he is ever going to treat you.

If a man yells and curses at you while you are dating, it is possible he will do it in the future. And it could escalate into abuse. If he is overly protective and jealous, take notice. If he makes fun of you or teases you and says he's only kidding, listen. He isn't. If he behaves in a way that makes you feel uncomfortable, listen to your gut feeling. The signs are always there. We are not always paying attention. Sometimes we see the signs, but we think we can change him or we make excuses. Stop! Ask yourself, "If he never changes this behavior, can I live with him the way he is?" Don't enter a relationship with the intention of changing a man. And don't make excuses for him when he tells you one thing and shows you another with his actions. That's who he truly is.

Take Settling Off the Table

If you're truly a woman of God, settling should never be an option. When you settle, you're telling God that you don't trust His plan; you are going to do things your way. Many women find themselves settling for relationships they know are wrong for them, but they stay because they fear being alone, fear starting over, or just feel pressure by loved ones or society.

When you have the wrong person occupying the space reserved for the right guy, you are making it impossible for the right guy to enter your life. You should let go of what is not right for you to make room for what God has in store for you. The moment you settle, the person who was meant for you comes along and you're no longer available to have him. It's like looking for a job—when you accept the first offer that comes along, suddenly better offers start rolling in, but now you're stuck.

So don't settle! Hold out for what you want and trust that God is going to deliver him.

CHAPTER 10

HOW TO KNOW HE'S THE RIGHT ONE TO DATE

HOW TO KNOW HE'S THE RIGHT ONE TO DATE

It can be hard to wait. You might want to give up and take what's readily available even if it's not what you want. We tell ourselves it's better than being alone or starting over. I've been there. There was a time in my life when I almost settled because I was tired of dating. I thought I could turn the wrong guy into the right guy if I worked hard and loved him enough. Most women have been there at some point in their dating life—you're with a guy you know is not the right one for you, but you justify staying with reasons why it's better than being alone. But there is another saying for that: "It's better to be alone and wish you were with someone than to be with someone and wish you were alone."

If you have been in a relationship for a while and you know it is not going anywhere, it can be hard to leave. Here are some steps to help you with the process of moving on when you're ready.

First, you should decide that this is not the relationship for you. Be honest. Be clear on why you are in this relationship. What is keeping you there? What would have to happen for you to leave? What attracted you to this person in the first place? What changed? What would leaving look like? What would staying look like? What is your gut telling you? Listen to your intuition and create a plan of action. Pray for strength and mentally separate yourself from the relationship. That is the hardest part. The rest will come to you once you're ready.

I've been in relationships where I've stayed much longer than I should have, but each relationship taught me something, and I applied those lessons to improve my next relationship. Ladies, we are strong and resilient. There's nothing stronger than a woman who has made up her mind. Just make sure you are making it up for something good.

*"There is no confusion when God sends
the right man into your life."*
—Emmanuela P. Rodenberg

Here are 5 steps to dating the right guy. You will know when you meet him. If you're unsure, then he is not the one. There is no confusion when it is right.

Step 1: The Pursuit

Allow him to pursue you! Do not chase a man. My husband was the first man I dated who I wanted to marry. It could have been that I was finally ready, but I believe it was because he was the one God created for me. With him, there was no confusion, no drama, no fear. It just felt right. From the very beginning, it was different than any other relationship I had been in. It was not an instant physical attraction which most people confuse as love. It developed slowly. We developed a friendship first. I wasn't sure he was interested in me other than as a friend! And I wasn't sure I was interested in him at first either. Both of us just enjoyed spending time with our mutual friends. We were enjoying our lives. That friendship was the beginning of our foundation.

I didn't know it at the time, but he was "checking me out" from day one. He chose to stay quiet about it for months. He was observing me and gathering information about me before he decided to ask me out. What finally got my attention was witnessing his integrity and his character. People think I'm boring when I say that, but it's the truth. He is a great guy with strong, honest character traits. He's not perfect. He's perfect for me. He has all the things that are important to me when it comes to sharing and building a life together.

When a man shows interest in you and is pursuing you, this is when you need to think about the list you made earlier. Ask yourself: Does he possess the characteristics I said were important to me in a mate? I'm not saying you should walk around with this book in your purse and pull it out every time a man approaches you! You should have your list in your head when you meet and go out with possible partners. This way you can quickly identify the ones who meet your requirements and the ones who don't.

Some people have a problem with me using the word "requirements". They think this type of woman is superficial or a snob. I would have to disagree with that because women should have standards. Men do. Too many women don't have standards. This is why women are accepting whatever a man throws at them. "Requirements" means you know what you want, and you can identify it when you see it. It means you are listening to God's will, you're smart, you've gotten to know yourself, and you can tell when a man might be one you should take some time to get to know.

Before dating my husband, I saw the qualities in him I knew I wanted in a husband. I wouldn't have been able to see those qualities so quickly if I didn't already know what was important to me in a future spouse. When a woman has standards, it tells the men in her life that she knows who she is and she's not going to accept just anyone. You don't always have to speak to get your points across. People, especially men, can tell a lot about you without you saying a word. Your behavior and demeanor can tell a person a lot about you. As women, we must be conscious about the messages we are sending.

Although we started out as friends and went out as a group for a long time, I could sense that our relationship was growing. When my future husband decided to pursue me, I allowed him. He asked me out on a proper date. I'm going to share with you the steps he took. This way you can see one good example of how a man should pursue a woman.

- My husband asked me out four days in advance. He was working out of town when he asked me out. He flew into town for the weekend to take me out on a date.

- He chose the restaurant and made the reservations.

- He picked me up, which I allowed because I knew him. (If you're meeting someone for the first time, it is a better idea to meet at the location if you're not comfortable with him picking you up).

- We both performed proper dating etiquette (dressing nicely, good table manners, etc.)

- I listened more than I spoke. I wanted to learn about who he was, so I allowed him to tell me. I let him lead the conversation. The first date is not the time to tell him your entire life story. Dating is discovering aspects of another person over time, not all at once. Be mysterious. Don't be evasive if he asks you a question, but don't divulge every little detail. Leave him curious. Be selective about what you tell a man in the beginning. He must earn the right to know you deeply. You can't go around sharing that part of yourself with everyone. Some conversations only need to be had in a committed relationship when you are certain he cares for you deeply and is there for the right reasons. Keep the conversation light and pleasant.

- He took care of the bill.

- I politely ended the date at a decent hour, letting him know I had church in the morning. I invited him to church, and he accepted. He has been going ever since.

Normally I don't advise asking a man out, but in this case, I felt good about it. I had known him for a while. It felt natural. This is my personal experience, but I hope you're finding valuable guidance.

Step 2: He Professes His Heart

As women, we are emotional beings. We are always ready to express our feelings when we feel them. The next part is hard to do, but it is necessary. You should give a man time to process how he feels about you. Sometimes it does not happen as fast as you would like, especially when you're head over heels. Be patient. Men and women process feelings in completely different ways. So, let him be the first to express his feelings to you before you profess your love for him. He must show he wants to commit his heart to you and be exclusive. Until you are exclusive, feel free to go out with other guys. You should have a life of your own, otherwise, you're going to sit around waiting for him to call and be disappointed when he doesn't. Show him you have a life. Show him you are busy, happy and fulfilled, and he will chase you down if he is interested.

Step 3: You Let Him Know Your Must-Haves and Non-Negotiables

Once he professes his love, it is time to let him know what it means to date you. What are your non-negotiables? Let him know where you are in your life, your goals, desires, and what is important to you. Don't sit him down and read him your lists! Tell him how much you appreciate that he expressed his feelings. Tell him he has the qualities you are looking for by giving him examples of ways he has shown you he is worthy. I made it clear to my husband I wanted a man who loved God and that I was ready for a serious relationship. I was not interested in playing games, and I meant it. Don't say it if you're not ready to back it up with your actions. I wasn't afraid of losing him—I was confident in who I was as a woman and I knew my value. I knew I was a prize for the right man. Men may not always respond to words, but they do respond to actions. Share your thoughts with him, and back them up with kind and self-assured behavior.

Step 4: Establish Ground Rules

Mutual understanding and shared expectations are critical for every relationship. Don't make assumptions because it only leads to disappointments. Discuss what is important and talk about each other's expectations. If you don't like something, speak up not just with your words but with your actions. Actions tend to speak louder than words. Show him what is acceptable and what is not. A person can only treat you the way you allow them to. Consistent follow-through is important in any relationship. Out of desperation, people often make empty threats to force their partners to comply, but it doesn't work long-term. After a while, you become a doormat. You won't be taken seriously. It can be hard sometimes, but it is crucial to follow through and do what you say you are going to do. Men will take you as seriously as you take yourself. They will respect you to the degree they see you respecting yourself.

Men tend to associate women with excessive talking. The best way to get a man's attention is through your actions. He should know you mean what you say. Don't say you're going to do something unless you plan to follow through. Period.

Step 5: Live in Your Truths–
Don't Compromise Your Core Values

"This above all: To thine own self be true."
—William Shakespeare

Never compromise who you are and your core values for a man, or anyone else for that matter. The man who was created for you by God will love you for who you are. He will not ask you to make compromises which go against your belief system. You won't have to pretend to be someone you are not just to keep him interested. He will cherish the woman you are now and the woman you continue to become. You must know your value and all that it encompasses. You are a miraculous woman of God with gifts and talents. You are a jewel and a treasure.

My husband and I spent an amazing two years dating. Psalm 25 says, "God confides in those that fear him." I didn't know what God was doing, but He told me in my heart and mind that this was my husband. I was sure about that, but I still held onto my convictions. I didn't want to marry a man who did not know and love God. I saw in my childhood what that lead to, and knew I didn't want that kind of life.

For two years, my husband willingly attended church with me. He did his soul searching. I remained true in my conviction to have a Godly husband. I showed him I would not marry a man who was not a man of God by keeping church in our relationship. Remember, people don't respond to words, they respond to actions.

As we continued to date, things progressed perfectly. He went to church with me. He flew me to Europe to meet his parents, and he met mine. We all loved each other. Then, my husband planned a romantic trip where he planned to propose to me. He planned the perfect evening, a lovely dinner, and a romantic walk on the beach. When the evening was ending, he got down on one knee, pulled out a little red box and asked if I would be his wife. I think he was sure I would say yes. But to his surprise and mine, I looked at him and asked, "Are you going to become a Christian?" He answered, "I can't promise you that." I said. "Then I can't marry you." He was shocked; I was shocked. So, the perfect evening wasn't so perfect after all.

I felt God telling me that is was going to be okay anyway. I believed and trusted God, and things worked out according to God's plan. My husband became a Christian after spending time soul-searching. He didn't do it for me. He did it when he established his convictions and understood what it meant to be a Godly man. Soon, he proposed again, and that time I said yes!

> *"And we know that in all things God works for the good of those who love him, who have been called according to his purpose."*
> *—Romans 8:28*

CHAPTER 11

THE ONLY PERSON YOU CAN CHANGE IS YOURSELF

THE ONLY PERSON YOU CAN CHANGE IS YOURSELF

It's hard to accept, but we can't change a man! Shocking, but that doesn't keep us from trying. Ladies, please know how important it is to understand only a man can change his life, and you can't do it for him. He should decide for himself. We cannot make a man do anything he does not want to do. He must have the motivation. People do things that are important to them. People also find excuses for avoiding the things they don't want to do. Ultimately, you must understand the only person you can change is yourself. So work on that. That should keep you busy for a while. When you change, the people in your life must decide if they want to be in your life or not. They will decide for themselves if they can live with the new you. They will either change to be with the new you or leave.

I made it clear to my husband that if he wanted a future with me, he had to make Christ his Lord. That was important to me. It was one of my non-negotiables. He said he understood and was going to work on it. He attended church with me every Sunday, and every Sunday I would ask him if he was ready. He would say he wasn't ready yet. So, I was waiting for him to meet this expectation but in his own time. I wanted him to give his life to Christ, but I also knew he needed to do it for himself. He needed to see the value in it for himself. My husband is a great guy, and anyone who knows him will tell you the same. He is loving, kind, and patient. But I was always reminded while we dated, that all those excellent qualities did not make him a man of God.

Sometimes it's hard to hear the truth, but it's necessary if we are going to have God-ordained relationships.

A Man of Integrity

A man of real character and integrity should be the qualities you desire in a husband. One thing I admire most about my husband is that he didn't make the most important decision of his life because of me. He could have taken that ring and offered it to a woman who had different standards. But he didn't. He accepted Christ on his own. As much as he loved me; he didn't do it for me, he did it for himself. Ultimately, God sent an amazing couple into our lives who studied the Bible with the both of us. We were both baptized and married a month later. Hollywood fairy tale? No. Beautiful, complicated, amazing and real? Yes.

I look back on our story and think about how different our lives would have been if I hadn't surrendered and allowed God to work in our lives. I could have just said "yes" on that beach and hoped for the best. I know now that I was a vessel God used to bring my husband into his kingdom. If I had compromised my values and mistrusted God, we wouldn't have the beautiful marriage we have today. I married a Godly man, and God is the center of our union.

CHAPTER 12

THE DECIDING FACTOR

THE DECIDING FACTOR

You never should worry about losing what God has created and ordained for you. What God has for you is for you. No one can take it away. So don't worry. Don't sacrifice who you are to keep a man. If he isn't for you, he will end up leaving anyway. Don't force yourself on anyone. Either a man will want you for you, all of you, or you are not meant to be with him. Be okay with that. You're not a match for everyone—you're only a match for the one God has chosen for you.

Be patient. It is not easy, I know. But remember that God is never late. His timing is always perfect. When you know who is ordering your steps and whom you belong to, you don't concern yourself with the small details of how things are going to happen. Trust that God has your perfect husband who He has prepared for you. Nothing you can do will change His mind about you and what He has in store for you.

You can delay things and take major detours by being impatient and trying to do things on your own instead of waiting on God. This is what happens to some who think God has forgotten about them and take matters into their own hands. They end up getting into relationships they had no business being in, marrying men God never intended for them to marry, creating families that end in divorce, causing generational chaos and heartache. All this can be prevented by waiting on God and remaining hopeful. You must believe without wavering. Remember the definition of faith and exercise it.

What Matters

"Charm is deceptive, beauty is fleeting; but a woman
who fears The Lord, will be greatly praised."
—Proverbs 31:30

Most men are attracted to a beautiful woman. An attractive woman can get a man's attention, but how does she keep it long-term? Many women rely solely on their physical appearance to attract and keep a man. It takes a whole lot more than physical beauty to keep a Godly man's attention.

A woman who is physically attractive is like a new car for a man. But just like everything else, the newness wears off eventually and it's what's under the hood that's going to keep the man interested in the long run. So, women, it's important you spend as much time on your inner beauty as you spend on your outer beauty. You take care of your nails, your hair, your clothes. But do you take care of your inner beauty? Are you kind, loving, compassionate, gentle, and respectful? These things matter to Godly men looking for a lifelong marriage. You may find yourselves so attracted to one another that you can't keep your hands off each other, but as your love grows, it's your mutual admiration and respect that will remain attractive to one another. So, let's not only strive for physical beauty; let's strive for inner beauty as well.

CHAPTER 13

LET A MAN BE A MAN

CHAPTER 13

LET A MAN BE A MAN

Choose your role carefully. There are a lot of hard-working, successful women out there who want to be married. Modern society has taught women to work hard and take care of themselves, so they won't "need" a man. They can do everything a man can do. These women are taught to be independent and hardworking, so they won't have to depend on a man for anything. The sad thing is while these women are working hard to be independent, a lot of men are doing the opposite. They are being lazy and not working hard to make something of themselves. Instead, they are looking for one of those strong, independent, hard working women to take care of them. Some women are essentially "paying" to have a man in their lives. They are asking men out, paying for dinners, taking them on trips, buying their clothes, and even paying their bills. All this to show their independence and success to men that's not even theirs. This behavior must stop, ladies. If you're going to be with a man, he should be able to provide for you financially along with your other needs.

A man can never truly be a man if you are covering all the responsibilities he needs to do for himself. You cannot "buy" a real man. A lazy man who wants to use you for your money or connections? Yes. But a man with integrity, will not allow you to support him financially. Real men take pride in being able to provide for their family. Do not allow yourself to be used by a man. Either he is ready for a woman in his life or he is not. You cannot make him ready by supporting him. He must realize he is not ready and get himself ready before he pursues a woman.

Who is to blame? Society? Women? Men? It's a combination. But since I'm speaking to women here, I will say we must change some of our current programming. The Bible doesn't say, "She who takes on a husband." Stop taking responsibility that was never assigned to you. You were created to be an aid. To be his aid, he must have a purpose. Your job is to support him while he is pursuing it. You are not the head of the relationship. You are not responsible for providing, he is. A man is supposed to provide and take care of a woman, not the other way around. Before a man enters a relationship, he should have a plan on how he is going to provide for his woman. It is not your job to volunteer to do his job for him. He should figure it out and share his vision with you. He should propose ways you can help him while he is busy providing for you. A man must know it is his job to love and provide for his family. It is your job to nurture, respect, and encourage your husband and your family.

There are exceptions. After you are married and he has spent time supporting you, making sure you are well cared for, you might find the dynamics of your family changes. Perhaps he loses his job. Or he goes back to school. Or you both decide your job earns more and he needs to care for an ailing parent. Every relationship is different. Situations arise, things change. The point is a man is supposed to be the primary provider for a woman. Don't try to use your influence, position, or income to lure a man into your life.

Before I ruffle any feathers, I am not saying women are subservient to men. I believe all people, men and women, should be respected as equal beings in society, in the home, and in the workplace. What I am saying here is speaking to the desperation some women feel that makes them trick a man into a relationship with money. This is not God's plan. It will fail every time. Men and women are meant to be partners in life. Both have their strengths and weaknesses, and together, they create a whole and healthy relationship.

I have always known I was going to do amazing work in the world and that financial success would follow. My prayer was always for God to bless me with my husband before I achieved my financial stability. I wanted no doubt that my husband was there because of his love for me and not for what I could provide financially. God answered my prayers. I know without a doubt my husband is here because of his love for me. Ten years into our relationship, he is supporting me as I work on my passion of becoming a full-time relationship advocate. He supports me emotionally, spiritually, physically, and financially. I have no doubt his intentions are pure.

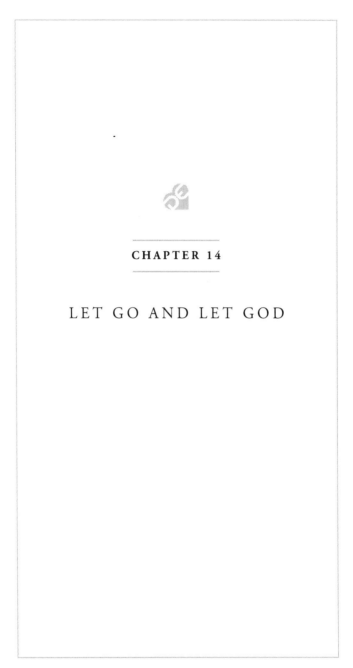

CHAPTER 14

LET GO AND LET GOD

CHAPTER 14

LET GO AND LET GOD

One of women's basic needs is to feel safe and secure. To have security, we tend to want to control things around us. We do things ourselves, or we feel they won't get done. We often take matters into our own hands that were never intended for us to handle. We try to manage every aspect of our love life. It should be planned, it should happen by a particular time, and it needs to be with this one particular guy. We put so much unnecessary pressure on ourselves that we can't enjoy the stage that we're in at the present moment.

We ignore our gut feelings and instincts and give up who we are for what we think we should have. We take on the role of the pursuer, we initiate contact, and make first moves to let men know we are interested. We ask men out to make sure it happens. We try to control everything, when the reality is, we simply need to let go and let God. We feel so burdened trying to make things happen when it should be happening naturally. Stop! Take control of the only person you have control over—you. Move out the way and let God be God, you might be surprised.

Fear and Love

Don't be afraid of losing something that belongs to you. If you are always on edge, you don't trust the person you're with, you are fearful he will leave you for someone else, you worry about what he's doing when he is not with you, or he doesn't do what he says he is going to do, then this is not the relationship God intended for you. You must practice letting go and let God take control of your life and your relationship. I promise you He knows what He is doing. He has been doing it for a long time. Relax and know that He has everything under control, nothing escapes His attention.

After you have committed to letting God guide you to your Godly husband, just continue living your life. Enjoying the blessings God has in front of you right now that you might be blind to because you are so focused on finding a husband. God is always going to do His part. The question that remains is—are you ready to do your part? I think you are! Be blessed and enjoy the journey of attracting your Godly husband.

The Final Challenge

- I challenge you to think about what it means to be married, how to choose the right man to commit to, and how to identify red flags.

- I challenge you to be the kind of woman that any man would be proud to call his wife.

- I challenge you to start with yourself and be happy before entering a relationship.

- I challenge you to know your value and know that you are a prize for the right man.

- I challenge you not to settle.

- I challenge you to be yourself.

- I challenge you to know what you stand for, know your core values and not compromise yourself for anyone.

Believe it is Possible

All of this means absolutely nothing if you do not believe you are worthy and deserving of having a Godly husband. We often do not get what we want because we don't think we deserve it. You are deserving and worthy of a Godly husband, and you need to keep telling yourself that over and over. You deserve a man who will accept and value you for exactly who you are. There is no reason to settle or compromise. Be firm with your core values and allow yourself to attract a man who will love you in the way you were created to be loved. You deserve the best. If you understand you are a precious gem, you are worthy, and you are attractive to your perfect mate, then you are a step closer to attracting your Godly husband.

Made in the USA
Columbia, SC
27 September 2023

23399179R00070